Ecosystems Research Journal

Great Lakes Research Journal

Ellen Rodger

CRABTREE
PUBLISHING COMPANY
WWW.CRABTREEBOOKS.COM

CRABTREE
PUBLISHING COMPANY
WWW.CRABTREEBOOKS.COM

Author: Ellen Rodger

Editors: Sonya Newland, Kathy Middleton

Design: Clare Nicholas

Cover design: Abigail Smith

Illustrator: Ron Dixon

Proofreader: Wendy Scavuzzo

Production coordinator and prepress technician: Tammy McGarr

Print coordinator: Katherine Berti

Produced for Crabtree Publishing Company by White-Thomson Publishing

Photo Credits:

Cover: Creative Commons: top left inset, bottom right inset; All other images from Shutterstock

Interior: Alamy: p. 11 Stiocktrek Images Inc., pp. 14–15 Aurora Photos, p. 16b Tom Uhlman, p. 19m All Canada Photos, p. 21t Robert La Salle/Aqua-Photo; Getty Images: p. 15m MCT; iStock: p. 9t Zofca, p.19t milehightraveler, p. 22l Phil Augustavo, p. 24l Velvetfish, p. 27b Sirimo, pp. 28–29 Mario Dias; Shutterstock: p. 4 Manfred Schmidt, p. 5t Krzysztof Winnik, p. 6t Le Do, p. 6b G. Bender, p. 7t Ken Schultze, p. 7b wwwarjag, p. 8b R. Maximiliane, pp. 8–9 Graham Taylor Photography, p. 10l Patthana Nirangkul, p. 10r SF Photo, pp. 10–11 lastdjedai, p. 12t Jon Nicholls Photography, p. 12b Brian E Kushner, p. 13l Zack Frank, p. 13r Morphart Creation, p. 14b Ryan M. Bolton, p. 15b Butterfly Hunter, p. 16t Simply Photos, p. 17 StevenRussellSmithPhotos, p. 18 Aivoges , p. 19b Ryan M. Bolton, p. 20 Sorayot Chinkanjanarot, p. 21b Galina Savina, p. 22r Abbie, p. 23 Steven Schremp, p. 24r Hein Nouwens, p. 25t Hank Erdmann, p. 25b moosehenderson, p. 26l 1082492116, p. 26r Vladimir Wrangel, p. 27t Morphart Creation, p. 29 ehrlif.

Library and Archives Canada Cataloguing in Publication

Rodger, Ellen, author
    Great Lakes research journal / Ellen Rodger.

(Ecosystems research journal)
Includes index.
Issued in print and electronic formats.
ISBN 978-0-7787-4658-4 (hardcover).--
ISBN 978-0-7787-4671-3 (softcover).--
ISBN 978-1-4271-2062-5 (HTML)

    1. Great Lakes (North America)--Juvenile literature. 2. Biotic communities--Great Lakes (North America)--Juvenile literature. 3. Lake ecology--Great Lakes (North America)--Juvenile literature. 4. Ecology--Great Lakes (North America)--Juvenile literature. I. Title.

QH104.5.G7R64 2018   j577.630977   C2017-907617-5
    C2017-907618-3

Library of Congress Cataloging-in-Publication Data

CIP Available at the Library of Congress

Crabtree Publishing Company
www.crabtreebooks.com   1-800-387-7650

Printed in the U.S.A./022018/CG20171220

Published in Canada
Crabtree Publishing
616 Welland Ave.
St. Catharines, Ontario
L2M 5V6

Published in the United States
Crabtree Publishing
PMB 59051
350 Fifth Avenue, 59th Floor
New York, New York 10118

Published in the United Kingdom
Crabtree Publishing
Maritime House
Basin Road North, Hove
BN41 1WR

Published in Australia
Crabtree Publishing
3 Charles Street
Coburg North
VIC, 3058

Contents

Mission to the Great Lakes   4

Field Journal Day 1: St. Lawrence River to the Bay of Quinte   6

Field Journal Day 2: Hamilton Harbour, Lake Ontario   8

Field Journal Day 3: Grimsby to Niagara River, Lake Ontario   10

Field Journal Day 4: Welland Canal to Lake Erie   12

Field Journal Day 5: Cleveland, Ohio, to Pelee Island, Ontario   14

Field Journal Day 6: Detroit River to St. Clair River   16

Field Journal Day 7: Lexington, Michigan, to Manitoulin Island, Ontario   18

Field Journal Day 8: Sault Ste. Marie, Ontario   20

Field Journal Day 9: Nipigon Bay, Ontario, to Isle Royale National Park, Michigan   22

Field Journal Day 10: Straits of Mackinac, Michigan, to Green Bay, Wisconsin   24

Field Journal Day 11: Milwaukee, Wisconsin, to Chicago, Illinois   26

Final Report   28

Your Turn   30

Learning More   31

Glossary & Index   32

Mission to the Great Lakes

Who wouldn't want to spend their summer on a lake? How about on five of the world's most fascinating lakes? As a **biologist**, my special interest is in freshwater lakes. I am traveling with a group of scientists studying North America's Great Lakes. We have been asked to write a report for the environmental organization Friends of the Lakes. We're heading out together on a research vessel from the lower St. Lawrence River. This river links to Lake Ontario in east-central Canada. From there, we will move west and visit sites on each lake.

The Great Lakes are 14,000 years old. They were formed when **glaciers** melted, leaving water to fill in the bowl-shaped depressions in the land.

I am hoping to see some lake sturgeon. These massive fish can weigh more than 200 pounds (90 kilograms).

The five Great Lakes make up the largest body of fresh water on Earth. Lake Michigan is located entirely within the United States. Lakes Superior, Huron, Ontario, and Erie are shared between the United States and Canada.

On my journey, I will examine environmental changes in and on the lakes. About 3,500 species of plants and animals, and 35 million people live within the lakes' **basin**. My investigation will focus on how **pollution** affects people and animals. I will also explore how shipping influences the environment, because the Great Lakes are a major transportation route.

The Great Lakes cover 750 miles (1,200 kilometers) from west to east.

CANADA

Nipigon Bay

Lake Superior

Sault Ste. Marie

Manitoulin Island

Straits of Mackinac

St. Lawrence River

Green Bay

Lake Huron

Bay of Quinte

Lake Michigan

Niagara Falls

Lake Ontario

St. Clair River

Lake St. Clair

Welland Canal

Milwaukee

Detroit

Detroit River

Lake Erie

Chicago

Cleveland

UNITED STATES

Field Journal: Day 1

St. Lawrence River to the Bay of Quinte

I boarded the research vessel on the St. Lawrence River. We traveled to Lake Ontario through a series of canals. Canals are channels or paths that connect the lake to other lakes. They are made by humans to allow big ships to travel easily. The Great Lakes are like superhighways for big cargo ships. More than 200 million tons (181 million metric tons) of goods are shipped this way each year.

Sightings

I spotted some purple loosestrife. This plant chokes out **native** plants on the edge of Lake Ontario.

Purple loosestrife

Some of the lakes are linked through human-made locks. Locks raise and lower ships. This allows ships to travel from the Atlantic Ocean, through the St. Lawrence River to the Great Lakes.

We sailed to the Bay of Quinte on the Canadian side of the lake. Our team spent a day helping farmers plant trees, shrubs, and grasses along the shoreline. Harmful algal blooms are common here. These happen when water is polluted by chemicals that are used to make plants grow. The chemicals seep into the lake from nearby farms. Bright blue-green blooms of algae can cover large areas and use up oxygen in the lake water. Without oxygen, fish and plants die.

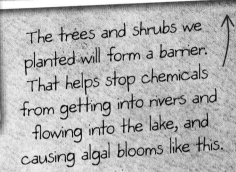

The trees and shrubs we planted will form a barrier. That helps stop chemicals from getting into rivers and flowing into the lake, and causing algal blooms like this.

natstat STATUS REPORT ST456/part B

Name: Walleye
(Sander vitreus)

Description:
Walleye is a freshwater fish. It is a fish that eats other fish. There is a small walleye fishery on Lake Ontario. Walleye are caught in big nets and traps.

Threats:
Occasional overfishing, high levels of toxic chemicals

Numbers: Unknown

Status:
The numbers of walleye began to decline in the 1970s because of water pollution. Programs to improve water quality helped walleye recover. The fish numbers declined again in the 1990s. Recently, water quality has improved again. About 100,000 young walleye have been released into the lake to increase the population. There are limits on how many walleye a fishing boat, or one person can catch.

7

Field Journal: Day 2

Hamilton Harbour, Lake Ontario

The glow from the steelmaking plants in the harbor lit up the night sky as we docked in Hamilton, Ontario. Pollution from factories here has created the largest **contaminated** site on the Canadian side of the Great Lakes. Poisonous chemicals have settled on the bottom of the harbor at Randle Reef. The reef is now being cleaned up. The goal is to make the area safe for wildlife again.

Many industries are located in Hamilton Harbour. They include steel makers, a sugar refinery, and grain and fertilizer storage. ↓

A barrier was built 20 years ago to keep common carp out of Cootes Paradise Marsh (see opposite). The carp is an **invasive species** from Asia. In 1996, 70,000 carp were in the marsh. The barrier has eliminated 95 percent of them.

Our team met with scientists from the Royal Botanical Gardens this afternoon. The Gardens controls a nearby **wetland** called Cootes Paradise Marsh. The marsh was once dying. Now it has been restored with plants such as cattails and wild rice. We saw several black-crowned night herons and white pelicans. We even saw a pair of bald eagles nesting. We were told this was the first nest seen on the lake in more than 45 years.

↑ Cormorants were among the many types of birds I saw nesting in Cootes Paradise.

Hamilton Harbour Remedial Action Plan: Ecosystem Recovery of Cootes Paradise

2010–15 plan and results

☑ Doubled aquatic vegetation to 324 acres (131 hectares) (target 667 acres (270 hectares))

☑ Improved water clarity from 14 to 24 inches (35 to 60 centimeters) (target 39 inches (100 centimeters))

2016–21 plan

☐ Marsh planting to lessen the impact of water level changes in lake

☐ Invasive plant management (removal) in marsh

☐ Repair shorelines

☐ Remove invasive common carp from the marsh

Field Journal: Day 3

Grimsby to Niagara River, Lake Ontario

Today, we headed back down Lake Ontario to the Niagara **Peninsula**. The peninsula juts down between Lake Ontario and Lake Erie. A bird expert told us that a "hawk watch" is held here each spring. Volunteers count **raptors** such as eagles, hawks, and kestrels during their annual spring **migration**. The count is one way that scientists study the environment. Plenty of raptors means a healthy ecosystem because there are many animals for them to eat.

Sightings

Using my binoculars, I was able to spot a golden eagle and two red-tailed hawks!

Golden eagle →

↑ The town of Niagara-on-the-Lake

I saw boats bringing tourists up the river to the base of Niagara Falls.

We traveled a little farther to see the Niagara River. This swirling river marks the border between Canada and the United States. The river flows from Lake Erie and exits here into Lake Ontario. The river is contaminated with chemicals from factories on both sides of the border. Both countries are working to clean up the river. They have cut the amount of chemicals that can be allowed to flow into the river. Habitats and wetlands near the river are being restored, but it will take some time before they are healthy again.

natstat STATUS REPORT ST456/part B

Name: American eel
(Anguilla rostrata)

Description:
The American eel is a fish with a long, snake-like body. American eels are born in the Atlantic Ocean and migrate to the Great Lakes through the St. Lawrence River.

Threats:
Dams and water barriers that prevent the eels from finding food, hydroelectric power stations, invasive species, water pollution

Numbers:
935,000 in 1985 to near 0 in 2001 (young eels in Lake Ontario)

Status: Endangered/at risk

Attach photograph here

Field Journal: Day 4

Welland Canal to Lake Erie

We spent a night going through the eight locks of the Welland Canal. They link Lake Erie to Lake Ontario. Lake Erie is 328 feet (100 meters) higher than Lake Ontario. Ships can't sail uphill easily, so they are raised or lowered inside a lock. Once we were out of the canal, we headed for Long Point—a long, narrow **sand spit**. We visited a marsh to see how scientists are trying to keep an invasive grass under control. The grass, *Phragmites australis*, can grow to 20 feet (6 meters) high. Scientists burn, crush, and use **herbicide** on the grass to prevent it from spreading.

Ships make their way to Lake Erie through a series of locks in the Welland Canal system.

Snapping turtle

Blanding's, spotted, and snapping turtles are some of the many species that live on Long Point. A special underwater tunnel was built to prevent turtles from being run over on the road.

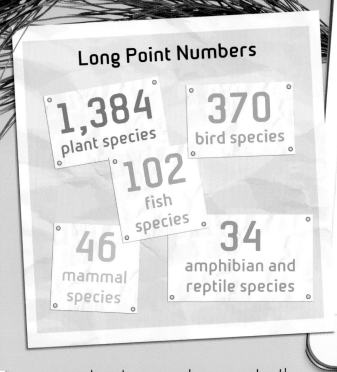

Long Point Numbers

1,384 plant species

370 bird species

102 fish species

46 mammal species

34 amphibian and reptile species

Fair weather gave us an easy crossing to Presque Isle State Park, near the port of Erie, Pennsylvania. Presque Isle is a sand spit, too. The dunes and grasses are home to birds, amphibians, and reptiles. The Atlantic flyway runs through here. It is a migratory path many birds follow to the Arctic where they breed. More than 300 species of birds stop at Presque Isle on their treks in the fall and spring.

Wind and wave action constantly change the shoreline and dunes of Presque Isle.

Sightings

Brilliant-orange Baltimore orioles nest on Presque Isle. I was lucky enough to see some of them.

Baltimore orioles

Field Journal: Day 5

Cleveland, Ohio, to Pelee Island, Ontario

We took samples of a bright-green algal bloom on the water near Cleveland, Ohio. Lake Erie is shallow and warm. Nearly 12.5 million people live around it in the United States and Canada. In the summer, pollution from industry and farm fertilizers creates toxic blooms. The water is harmful to drink or swim in. Governments in Canada and the United States have agreed to limit pollution and the use of farm fertilizers. This will help prevent the blooms.

A toxic Lake Erie algal bloom in 2014 left 500,000 people near Toledo, Ohio without drinking water for weeks.

natstat STATUS REPORT ST456/part B

Name: Lake Erie watersnake
(Nerodia sipedon insularum)

Description:
Lake Erie watersnakes are non–venomous snakes found only on a few islands in Lake Erie. They spend most of their time in or near the water, preying on fish or amphibians.

Threats:
Hunting, habitat loss due to clearing vegetation from shores

Numbers: 3,470

Status:
Special concern

Attach photograph here

We devoted most of the day to birdwatching. Our first stop was Kelleys Island State Park. Kelleys is part of a group of small islands in Ohio. It is in the middle of two bird migration routes. Hundreds of species of birds rest here. Our second stop was the largest island in Lake Erie—Pelee Island. There is an observatory here that collects information on bird migration. We learned that about 40 breeding pairs of Acadian flycatchers make their home in the island's forest.

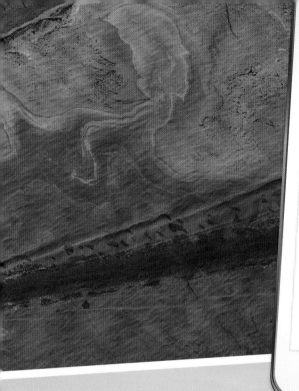

All the Great Lakes are used for summertime recreation. Bacteria levels are monitored on the beaches, like this one at Kelleys Island State Park. People are warned not to swim when the ← levels are too high.

Point Pelee is a point of land that juts out into Lake Erie close to Pelee Island. Millions of monarch butterflies stop here each fall on their annual migration south to Mexico.

← Monarch butterflies →

Field Journal: Day 6

Detroit River to St. Clair River

We set off north on one of the busiest shipping routes in North America. The Detroit River joins Lake St. Clair. The lake links to the St. Clair River and on to Lake Huron. In the 1960s, the Detroit River was one of the most polluted rivers in the United States and Canada. Lake Erie was also considered "dead" from algal blooms. In the 1970s, clean water laws were passed. Industries were forced to reduce the chemical waste dumped into the river. Decades of cleanup has improved water quality, but there is still much to do.

Several islands in the Detroit River and coastal wetlands are part of the Detroit River International **Wildlife Refuge.**

I spotted a muskrat lodge near Grassy Island. Grassy is a Detroit River island that used to be a dump for toxic soil from industrial sites.

The area around Lake St. Clair in the Great Lakes system is known as a waterfowl staging area. This is a place where birds rest while migrating.

Peak total for spring migration: 60,000
Peak total for fall migration: 150,000

We were invited to meet with an ecologist from the Walpole Island First Nation reserve. The members of the nation call the island Bkejwanong. It is located on a stretch of water between the St. Clair River and Lake Huron. A major **petrochemical** industry is located nearby. There is also a lot of ship traffic on the river. Walpole Island has many rare ecosystems. People avoid trampling through tallgrass **prairies** so they don't damage rare plant species. They also look for ways to conserve their forests and **savannas**.

↑
Southern flying squirrel

Southern flying squirrels and northern bobwhite quails are species at risk that live on Walpole Island. It is also a summer nesting area for purple martins.

Field Journal: Day 7

Lexington, Michigan, to Manitoulin Island, Ontario

Today, we had a look beneath the surface of Lake Huron. We went scuba diving in the underwater forest near Lexington, Michigan. This forest is located 40–50 feet (12–15 meters) under water. It was discovered by divers in the 1980s. Only fragile 7,000-year-old tree stumps and broken logs remain. Scientists think it was a swamp forest of cedar and pine trees that was preserved when glaciers melted and water covered it completely.

Lake Huron is the second-largest Great Lake. It has the longest shoreline, at 3,827 miles (6,160 kilometers).

We headed to Bruce Peninsula National Park, a finger of land between the lake and Georgian Bay. Some of the trees in the ancient living forests here are 1,000 years old.

We kept an eye out for Massassauga rattlesnakes, a threatened venomous snake native to this region.

We sailed north to Manitoulin Island in Ontario and met with conservationists who are trying to protect this island habitat. Manitoulin is the largest island in a lake in the world. It has 108 of its own lakes—and some of these even have their own islands! The conservationists there showed us several alvar habitats. Alvars are areas of rock with thin or no soil covering. Many alvars had rare plants and animals living on them. In fact, some lichens cannot be found anywhere else in the world.

Creeping juniper growing on an alvar area on Manitoulin Island

natstat STATUS REPORT ST456/part B

Name: Spotted turtle
(Clemmys guttata)

Description:
This is a small turtle, growing up to around 4.5 inches (11 centimeters). It has a smooth black shell with yellow-orange spots. It lives in marshes and bogs.

Threats:
Habitat loss and accidental crushing on roads; predators also love turtle eggs

Numbers: 24 (estimated)

Status: Endangered

Attach photograph here

Field Journal: Day 8

Sault Ste. Marie, Ontario

On our way to Lake Superior, we saw a storm brewing as we traveled through the locks at Sault Ste. Marie. Every year, about 10,000 ships pass through the locks on their way to and from Lake Superior. The largest ships are more than 1,000 feet (330 meters) long. They can carry 70,000 tons (63,500 metric tons) of **iron ore** or thousands of tons of grain. Our vessel is small in comparison. We knew we needed to head quickly for a bay where we could take shelter. The waves in a storm in Lake Superior can reach 40 feet (12 meters) high!

Superior is the largest of the Great Lakes, as well as the largest freshwater lake in the world.

SPECIES IN LAKE SUPERIOR

Plants	59
Bottom-dwelling invertebrates	28
Fish	26
Small plankton	25
Parasites	10
Insects	2

Lake Superior sits higher up than the other lakes, and its waters empty into Lakes Huron, Erie, and Ontario. In each lake we visited, I noticed the water was high. This year, water levels were the highest ever on record for Lake Ontario and Lake Erie. The high water was caused by a very rainy spring. Cold winters also mean more ice on the lakes, and in rivers and streams that flow into the lakes. Scientists think that **global warming** contributes to the rising lake levels through more severe storms and rain.

I caught a glimpse of a muskellunge fish at the bottom of a bay. →

STATUS REPORT ST456/part B

Name: Lake sturgeon
(Acipenser fulvescens)

Description:

A sturgeon is a massive freshwater fish. It can weigh up to 400 pounds (180 kilograms) and measure more than 6.5 feet (2 meters) long. It is light brown to gray, with a long snout and organs that look like whiskers near its mouth. Sturgeon can live for more than 100 years.

Attach photograph here

Threats:
Overfishing, habitat loss, poor water quality, and barriers such as dams have made it difficult for the fish to move and reproduce.

Numbers: Unknown

Status:
Threatened/at risk in the Great Lakes

21

Field Journal: Day 9

Nipigon Bay, Ontario, to Isle Royale National Park, Michigan

Lake Superior was calm and clear today after the recent storm. We passed where the Nipigon River meets the lake. This is Lake Superior's largest **tributary** river. It has several hydro dams for making electricity. I can see that a lot of the forest here has been cut down. The trees were used to make paper products at paper mills. Most mills are now closed, but the water is still polluted. Since 1987, government and industry in the area have been trying to restore the environment.

A power plant on Lake Superior

Sightings

There's nothing like a giant moose to make you stop in your tracks! Moose are not native to the island. They are thought to have been brought here by hunting clubs in the early 1900s.

Moose

I spent the rest of the day swatting away mosquitoes and listening to frogs on Isle Royale National Park in Michigan. Our team took part in a frog count. We placed "frog logger" recorders in wetland habitats. These areas are watched from spring to fall. Frogs and other amphibians are sensitive to environmental changes such as **climate change** and pollution. The U.S. National Park Service has several monitoring programs on Isle Royale. These programs study bats, songbirds, water quality, climate, and mercury contamination.

Great Lake Sizes and Depths

Great Lake	Size (water area)	Maximum Depth (measure at low water)
Lake Superior	31,700 sq. miles (82,102 sq. km)	1,332 ft (406 m)
Lake Huron	23,000 sq. miles (59,570 sq. km)	751 ft (229 m)
Lake Michigan	22,300 sq. miles (57,757 sq. km)	925 ft (282 m)
Lake Erie	9,190 sq. miles (23,802 sq. km)	210 ft (64 m)
Lake Ontario	7,340 sq. miles (19,011 sq. km)	804 ft (245 m)

A lighthouse on Isle Royale ↓

Field Journal: Day 10

Straits of Mackinac, Michigan, to Green Bay, Wisconsin

Today, we went shipwreck diving in Lake Michigan at the Straits of Mackinac Shipwreck Preserve. The straights are the waterways that connect Lake Huron to Lake Michigan. They have been shipping lanes for hundreds of years, but the currents here are tricky. Dozens of sunken ships lie at the bottom, with the earliest known dating to 1856. Now the wrecks are littered with the shells of zebra mussels and quagga mussels. These invasive species attach to the ships' hulls and slowly rot them.

Sightings

Herring gulls nest on the islands at the tip of Wisconsin's Door Peninsula, which separates Green Bay from Lake Michigan.

Herring gull →

There are more than 6,000 shipwrecks in ← the Great Lakes.

I watched
the Sun set over
Green Bay.

I couldn't believe my eyes as we sailed into Green Bay in Wisconsin. A giant algal bloom had turned the water into a brilliant green soup. Blooms are common on this inlet of Lake Michigan. They sometimes create "dead zones" in the water. Dead zones are areas where the blooms sink to the bottom of the cold lake water and suck all the oxygen out. With no oxygen to breathe, fish suffocate and die. In 2014, a bloom killed so many that the shore was thick with rotting fish.

natstat STATUS REPORT ST456/part B

Name: Piping plover
(Charadrius melodus)

Description:
The piping plover is a small shorebird that nests on open beaches on the shores of the Great Lakes. Its sandy gray color helps it blend into its beach environment.

Threats:
Humans disturbing nests and changing beach ecosystems by building nearby

Numbers: 68 nesting pairs (2016)

Status: Endangered/at risk

Attach photograph here ➤

Field Journal: Day 11

Milwaukee, Wisconsin, to Chicago, Illinois

This morning, a fisher from Milwaukee, Wisconsin, took us out to his old fishing grounds, three hours from shore. He no longer goes fishing there. No one does. There is no fishing industry in this part of Lake Michigan because there are not enough fish. Invasive species such as sea lampreys and quagga mussels have destroyed the habitat for native fish. There are 180 invasive species in the Great Lakes. Asian carp are the next big threat.

Zebra mussels are an invasive species in this area.

↓

INVASIVE SPECIES

Species: Asian carp

How it harms:
Eats all the **plankton**, leaving nothing for native fish to eat

Where:
Moving up the Mississippi River System. Some have been found in Lake Michigan. The carp were introduced to help clean fish farm ponds, but some escaped.

Protection measures:
1) Electric barriers in the Chicago Sanitary and Ship Canal 37 miles (60 kilometers) from Lake Michigan

2) New laws that require ships to have equipment that sterilizes ballast waters and prevents invasive species from getting into the lakes

Asian carp ↗

We made it to Chicago, the final stop on our Great Lakes tour. I took the kayak out on the lake. The water was incredibly clear. Quagga mussels have eaten all the plankton. They filter the water and this is why I could see down several feet. Clear water in a Great Lake doesn't mean clean and healthy. In this case, it means species that once lived here are now dead. The entire ecosystem has changed from what it was 100, or even 20 years ago. And it is still changing.

Lake Michigan means "great water." This Great Lake is the only one located entirely in the United States. Twelve million people share its shores in four states: Wisconsin, Illinois, Indiana, and Michigan.

Sightings

I spotted a river otter playing. Their webbed feet help them swim well. They love to eat fish and turtles.

River otter →

The lake water around Chicago is very clear. ↓

Final Report

REPORT TO:
FRIENDS OF THE LAKES

OBSERVATIONS

This trip has shown me two important things:

1) The truly enormous size of the Great Lakes.
2) Their importance to human, animal, and plant life in North America.

These lakes contain nearly 20 percent of all the fresh water in the world. The lakes have been changed by human use. Industries in both the United States and Canada depend on them for transporting goods and materials for manufacturing. The cities and towns on and around the Great Lakes all need the lakes to survive. They use lake water for drinking, industry, electricity, farming, fishing, recreation, and tourism.

Clean water laws have helped improve water quality, and set standards for shipping companies, industries, and individuals using the lakes.

FUTURE CONCERNS

The growth of cities around the Great Lakes is shrinking natural habitats for plants and animals. The increased human population is overwhelming the safety measures put into place years ago. Algal blooms are once again threatening animal and plant life on the lakes. Invasive species change habitats in and around the lakes. Changing water levels are causing flooding, and damaging shorelines and property.

CONSERVATION PROJECTS

The United States and Canada share the responsibility of protecting the Great Lakes environment. History has shown that when the two countries work together, it helps the lakes survive and thrive. Laws are being updated to deal with environmental threats. Community volunteers are also making efforts by holding cleanup days along shorelines, and planting native trees and grasses. Conservation groups are reintroducing native animals back into the lakes. The United Nations has also identified several areas around the Great Lakes as **Biosphere Reserves** that need protecting. Lake conservation needs constant effort. We have to continually do what's right for lake ecosystems.

Scientists believe that global warming will mean less winter ice cover on the lakes, warmer waters in the summer, and more storms.

Your Turn

★ Do you live near a Great Lake? How about a smaller lake, river, or creek? You can learn about the body of water you live near by doing research. Learn about ecosystems by reading books at your library. Ask your librarian where you can find information. Often, they can direct you to a good source.

★ Once you have done your research, write your own report about the body of water. You might want to include these things: 1) A map of the body of water. 2) Details on its history. 3) A list of plants and animals that are part of its ecosystem.

★ Is it possible to visit this body of water? If so, go with a parent or guardian. Bring a camera and take pictures of the water and shore. Make notes in a journal about any animals or plants you see. Is the shoreline sandy or rocky? No fact is unimportant. Add this information and some images to your report.

★ In your report, write at least one new thing you have learned about your local body of water. Even if it is just a note about rocks or water color, you have paid attention and made an observation.

Learning More

BOOKS

Paddle-to-the-Sea by Holling C. Holling (HMH Books for Young Readers, 1980)

The Great Lakes by Janet Piehl (Lerner Publishing, 2010)

Where Is Niagara Falls? by Megan Stine (Grosset & Dunlap, 2015)

WEBSITES

www.ducksters.com/geography/lakes.php
Learn about lakes and large bodies of water all over the world and how they compare to the Great Lakes.

www.enwin.com/kids/water/the_great_lakes.cfm
Learn basic facts about the Great Lakes and water conservation.

http://sciencewithkids.com/science-facts/facts-about-the-great-lakes.html
This page gives information along with a map of the Great Lakes and photos of lakeshores.

Glossary & Index

ballast heavy materials that are put on ships to increase their weight

basin an area drained by a lake or many lakes

biologist a scientist who studies living things

Biosphere Reserves ecosystems that are considered special or rare and that are protected from harm

climate change a change in climate patterns all over the world, usually linked to the increased use of fossil fuels such as oil and gas

contaminated impure or unsafe

ecosystem a community of plants and animals living in the same area

glaciers frozen rivers of ice that are moving slowly

global warming the gradual warming of Earth's atmosphere

herbicide chemicals put on plants to kill weeds

invasive species a plant or animal that has spread to an environment that is not its natural habitat

iron ore rock that contains iron

low water time when water is at its lowest level

migration the seasonal movement of animals from one region to another

native born or occurring naturally in an area

peninsula land that sticks out into a body of water, so that it is almost surrounded

petrochemical of or relating to chemicals and other products made from oil and natural gas

plankton tiny life forms that float in fresh water, which fish and other animals eat

pollution when an environment is harmed or made dirty by chemicals or other substances

prairies areas of open grassland

raptors birds of prey, or birds that eat other animals

sand spit a piece of land formed over time by waves that dump sand and soil

savannas grassy plains with few trees

tributary a smaller river or stream that flows into a large river or lake

wetland a marsh or swamp surrounding a lake

wildlife refuge a place where wild animals are protected, or where their habitat is protected

algal blooms 7, 14, 16, 29
American eels 11

Baltimore orioles 13
Bay of Quinte 5, 7
Bruce Peninsula 18
butterflies 15

carp 8, 9, 26
chemicals 7, 8, 11, 16
Cootes Paradise Marsh 8, 9

Detroit River 5, 16

glaciers 4, 18
global warming 21, 29

golden eagles 10
grasses 7, 12, 13, 29
Green Bay 5, 24, 25

habitat loss 14, 19, 21
Hamilton Harbour 8
herring gulls 24

industries 8, 14, 16, 22, 28
invasive species 8, 11, 24, 26, 29
Isle Royale 22, 23

Kelleys Island 15

Lake Erie 5, 10, 11, 12, 14, 15, 21, 23

Lake Huron 5, 16, 17, 18, 21, 23
Lake Michigan 5, 23, 24, 25, 26, 27
Lake Ontario 4, 5, 6, 7, 10, 11, 12, 21, 23
Lake St. Clair 16, 17
lake sturgeon 5, 21
Lake Superior 5, 20, 21, 23
laws 16, 26, 28, 29
locks 6, 12, 20
Long Point 12

Manitoulin Island 5, 18, 19
migration 10, 11, 13, 15
moose 22

Niagara Falls 5, 11
Niagara River 10, 11
Nipigon Bay 5, 22
northern bobwhite quails 17

overfishing 7, 21

Pelee Island 14, 15
piping plovers 25
pollution 5, 7, 8, 11, 14, 16, 22, 23
Presque Isle 13
purple loosestrife 6

quagga mussels 24, 26, 27

red-tailed hawks 10

river otters 27

Sault Ste. Marie 5, 20
shipping 5, 6, 12, 16, 17, 20, 24, 28
shipwrecks 24
St. Clair River 5, 16, 17
St. Lawrence River 4, 5, 6, 11
Straits of Mackinac 5, 24

walleye 7
Walpole Island 17
Welland Canal 5, 12
wetlands 9, 11, 16, 23

zebra mussels 24

X-MEN

AN ORIGIN STORY

Based on the Marvel comic book series The X-Men
Adapted by Rich Thomas Jr.
Illustrated by Pat Olliffe *and Hi-Fi Design*

New York • Los Angeles

MARVEL
marvelkids.com

© 2014 MARVEL

Published by Marvel Press, an imprint of Disney Book Group. No part of this book may be
reproduced or transmitted in any form or by any means, electronic or mechanical, including
photocopying, recording, or by any information storage and retrieval system, without written
permission from the publisher. For information address Marvel Press, 1101 Flower Street,
Glendale, CA 91201.

Case illustrated by Pat Olliffe and Brian Miller
Designed by Stuart Smith

Printed in the United States of America
Second Edition
1 3 5 7 9 10 8 6 4 2
G942-9090-6-14060
ISBN 978-1-4231-7226-0

Did you ever have a dream that felt so real—

that you were sure you weren't dreaming at all?

This is a story about a boy named **Charles Xavier**, who dreame
he could do many things an ordinary boy could not do.

Did you ever have a dream that felt so real—

that you were sure you weren't **dreaming** at all?

This is a story about a boy named **CHARLES XAVIER**, who dreamed he could do many things an ordinary boy could not do.

He dreamed his mind could leave his body and float like a feather.

He dreamed he could know what other people were thinking before they even opened their mouths to speak.

But Charles didn't want to tell other people about his special dreams, because he was afraid of how they would react.

So Charles dreamed of a world where people like him—people who felt different— could be proud to be themselves.

But those dreams would always end.

You see, the world didn't seem like a very fair place to Charles. His father had passed away when he was just a young boy.

He lived in his father's mansion with his mother, who loved him very much.

But his older brother and his stepfather lived in the mansion as well. And they were heartless and cruel to Charles and his mother.

Charles had always heard whispers of things that no one was saying out loud. The kids at school would often make fun of Charles for hearing things.

But as Charles grew older he began to hear the voices clearer and clearer. Eventually he realized that he could read minds!

As time went by and Charles grew older, he used his gift to gain knowledge.

He studied to become a doctor of science. He wanted to learn more about why he had these special powers.

Charles soon discovered that he was a mutant—**a person born with special abilities** that made them different from everyone else. Then Charles became more curious than ever. He wanted to meet others like him.

His studies took him around the world. On one trip, Charles met another mutant. But this man did not want to use his powers for good.

This mutant was **evil**, and
Charles had to stop him. So
they fought on the astral plane.

And Charles defeated him.

Charles believed a mutant's
gifts were meant to help
mankind, not harm it.

Charles soon met another mutant—a man named **ERIK MAGNUS**.

Magnus had the mutant power to move metal objects without touching them. Charles and Magnus became fast friends. But they did not always agree.

Magnus knew humans feared and hated mutants.

He thought the only way for mutants to keep themselves safe was to use their power to take over the world.

But Charles still dreamed of a world where humans and mutants could live together peacefully.

Then Charles and Magnus met and defeated an evil human named **BARON VON STRUCKER**, who wanted to use his wealth to destroy anyone he didn't like, and Magnus felt that this proved humans were bad.

He took the Baron's gold and flew away with it, telling Charles he was foolish to believe that mankind was good.

Charles was sad to lose his friend. As he continued his journey, he began to think about returning home.

He could use his father's fortune to find mutants and make sure that anyone born with special powers used them to help mankind.

But during a stop on his journey home, Charles encountered a new threat. This one came from another world.

An alien named **Lucifer** wanted to destroy both humans **and** mutants. He and Charles fought. Lucifer collapsed his secret hideaway on top of Charles. Charles survived, but his legs had been crushed. He would never be able to walk again.

He returned home, more determined than ever to find other mutants. He would train them to fight any threat— mutant, human, or alien.

His mother and stepfather had passed away and his brother had left the mansion long ago. The Xavier home was empty, but it wouldn't stay that way for long.

The first mutant Charles found
was named **SCOTT SUMMERS**.
Charles called him Cyclops for
the optic blast he could shoot
from his eyes.

Next, Charles and Cyclops
rescued a teenager from an
angry mob that hated mutants.
The boy, **BOBBY DRAKE**, could
turn himself into ice and called
himself Iceman.

The growing group next found **WARREN WORTHINGTON III**, who called himself Angel for the wings that helped him fly.

And finally **HANK McCOY** joined the group. Hank was called The Beast because of his large hands and feet, which helped him swing like a monkey and punch like a gorilla!

Charles renamed the mansion Xavier's School for Gifted Youngsters. To the world it was just another boarding school. But secretly, it was a place where young mutants could learn to use their powers. The students were given uniforms and each pledged to fight for Charles's dream.

Charles called himself Professor X and his team the X-Men, because each member had an extraordinary power.

The X-Men soon welcomed their fifth and final founding member—
JEAN GREY, called Marvel Girl! Jean could move things with
her mind.

Professor X then built a device to locate other mutants. The
computer, called Cerebro, showed that a mutant was attacking
an army base at Cape Citadel.

It was the professor's old friend Magnus!

Now known as **Magneto**, he
had begun to wage his war
on the human race.

Charles knew that only his
X-Men could stop him!

The X-Men arrived at Cape Citadel shortly after Magneto had begun to attack.

The X-Men sprang into action—and attacked him right back.

Cyclops tried to **blast** through Magneto's magnetic field.
But he couldn't.

Magneto guided every
missile that Marvel
Girl tried to send at
him right back at her.

Angel and The Beast did not fare much better.

At last, Magneto attacked them all. But Marvel Girl covered her teammates with a force field.

The X-Men were not so easily defeated!

The X-Men had
driven off Magneto.
But they had come
to stop Magneto and
turn him over to the
police. And in that
they had failed.

The X-Men were disappointed. But Professor X was proud of them.
Magneto was a most powerful mutant, and they had foiled his attack.

Over the next few months, the X-Men trained in a special room called the Danger Room. The room was filled with obstacles to help the X-Men perfect their abilities.

And Professor X used Cerebro to keep a constant watch for new mutants.

And he found many!
But more often than not
the mutants were evil.

Magneto assembled these evil mutants into his
own group called the **Brotherhood**.

More mutants were appearing each day. And humans were becoming more and more concerned. They were afraid of mutant powers. Even though the X-Men tried to protect humans and live Professor Xavier's dream, people treated all mutants badly.

And as the evil mutants grew in number, so did the X-Men. Cyclops's brother **ALEX SUMMERS**, the energy-blasting mutant called Havok, and **LORNA DANE**, called Polaris for her magnetic abilities, joined the team.

But their group was still too small to fight all of the threats. And when the X-Men went missing on a dangerous mission, Professor X searched the globe and assembled a new group to rescue them.

In Canada, he recruited the mutant named Wolverine, who could heal himself of any injury and whose claws could cut through almost anything!

In Germany, Charles rescued KURT WAGNER, called Nightcrawler, who could move from place to place with just a thought.

In Ireland, Charles found **SEAN CASSIDY**—Banshee—whose sonic scream could shatter stone and steel.

In Africa, Charles met **ORORO MUNROE**, a weather mutant called Storm.

And in Russia, the mutant Peter Rasputin, called Colossus because he could turn himself to metal, bade farewell to his family to join the professor.

In Japan, Sunfire, whose powerful blasts were as hot as the sun, joined the professor.

And finally, in the American west, JOHN PROUDSTAR left his reservation to join the X-Men!

Charles's new
international team wasted
no time in it's search to
find the Original X-Men.

The new X-Men rescued
the original team, and
working together, both
teams defeated Krakoa,
the living island!

When the new group returned, they decided to stay at Xavier's school.

They trained to use their powers. And soon they became full-fledged **X-Men**, and a kind of family.

But no matter what the X-Men did . . .

. . . trouble seemed to find them.

No matter what day, month, or season . . .

. . . the X-Men were never safe.

Enemies both new and old were always attacking.

And with every incident, humans became more worried
about mutants.

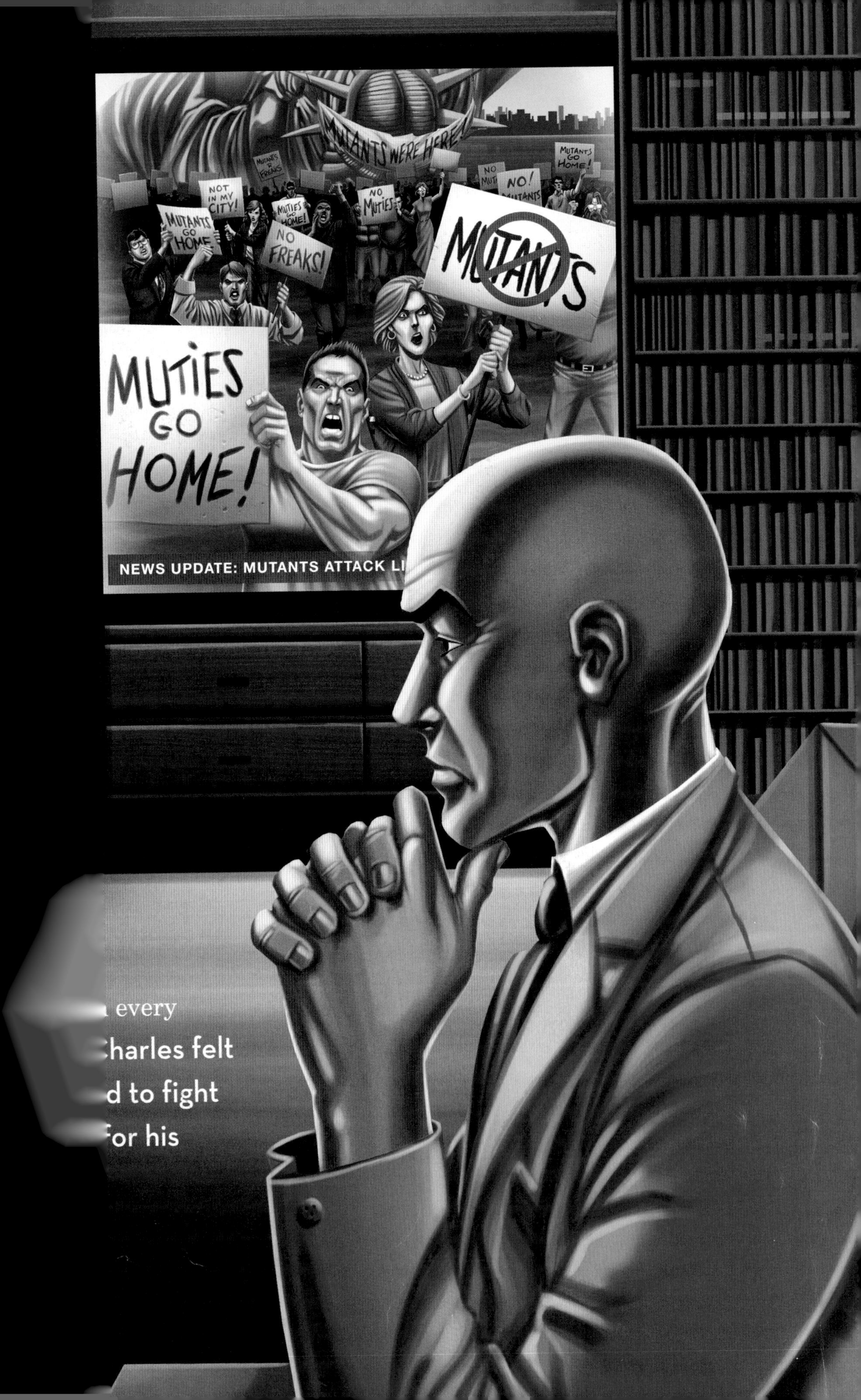

MUTANTS WERE HERE!

NOT IN MY CITY!

MUTANTS GO HOME

MUTIES GO HOME!

NO FREAKS!

NO MUTIES

NO! MUTANTS

MUTANTS GO HOME

MUTANTS

MUTIES GO HOME!

NEWS UPDATE: MUTANTS ATTACK LI

...a every
...Charles felt
...d to fight
...for his

And whenever Charles felt hope leaving him,

he'd lay down just as he did when he was a boy,

close his eyes, drift off to sleep . . .

...and dream.